THE
PSALMS
AROUND
US

COUNTRYSIDE PRESS
Farm Journal, Inc., Philadelphia, Pa.

DOUBLEDAY & COMPANY, INC.
GARDEN CITY, NEW YORK

Quotations from the Psalms are from the
Revised Standard version of the Bible, used by permission

Published by Countryside Press, a division of Farm Journal, Inc.,
Washington Square, Philadelphia, Pennsylvania

Copyright ©, by Farm Journal, Inc., 1970
All rights reserved

Library of Congress catalog card number 72-114340

Photographs in this book are by Grant Heilman, except
those on pages 9 and 10, courtesy of NASA

Book design: Al J. Reagan

Distributed to the book trade by Doubleday & Company, Inc.,
Garden City, New York

CONTENTS

On earth
as in heaven

Three thousand years ago in a different language in a far country, another human being asked, like the astronaut, *What is man that thou art mindful of him?* In his kinship with the universe, David marveled *Thou hast made man little less than God.* He looked around him at the rich beauty, the glory, the power of the *earth given to the sons of men* and put his feelings into words—psalms.

The dialogue between the inner better self of Everyman and his God is eternal. His pride at walking on the moon is tempered with a new sense of divinity.

We scan with new wonder the familiar vistas; we see a hill, a tree, a bud in sharper relief. Shaken by a new view of heaven, we need the reassurance of the earth.

Beautiful scenes . . . the bounty and artistry of the universe . . . inspire our best thoughts and, subsequently, deeds. As steel towers rise to compete with the glacier-carved hills, as swaths of concrete crowd back the fresh, yielding earth, nature's beauty becomes more precious.

We have collected in this book scenes from our country and our time. The words which they illustrate anew will forever be timeless.

THE HEAVENS TELL THE GLORY OF GOD

W hen I look at thy heavens, the
work of thy fingers,
the moon and the stars which
thou hast established;
what is man that thou art mindful
of him,
and the son of man that thou
dost care for him?   8:3,4

Yet thou hast made him little less
  than God,
and dost crown him with glory
  and honor.   8:5

O give thanks to the Lord,
    for he is good,
      for his steadfast love endures for
        ever.
To him who made the great lights,
    for his steadfast love endures for
      ever;
the sun to rule over the day,
    for his steadfast love endures for
      ever;
the moon and stars to rule over
      the night,
    for his steadfast love endures for
    ever   136:1,7-9

The heavens are telling the
    glory of God;
    and the firmament proclaims his
    handiwork.
In them he has set a tent for the
    sun,
which comes forth like a bride-
    groom leaving his chamber,
    and like a strong man runs its
    course with joy.
Its rising is from the end of the
    heavens,
    and its circuit to the end of them;
    and there is nothing hid from its
    heat.   19:1,4-6

For I know that the Lord is great,
  and that our Lord is above all
    gods.
Whatever the Lord pleases he
  does,
  in heaven and on earth,
  in the seas and all deeps.
He it is who makes the clouds rise
    at the end of the earth,
  who makes lightnings for the
    rain
  and brings forth the wind from
    his storehouses.   135:5-7

The clouds poured out water;
  the skies gave forth thunder;
  thy arrows flashed on every side.
The crash of thy thunder was in
    the whirlwind;
  thy lightnings lighted up the
    world;
  the earth trembled and shook.   77:17,18

The heavens proclaim his righteousness;
and all the peoples behold his glory.   97:6

THE EARTH
IS THE LORD'S
AND
THE FULNESS THEREOF

The earth is the Lord's and
    the fulness thereof,
    the world and those who dwell
    therein;
for he has founded it upon the seas,
    and established it upon the rivers.
Who shall ascend the hill of the
    Lord?
    And who shall stand in his holy
    place?
He who has clean hands and a pure
    heart,

who does not lift up his soul to
    what is false,
and does not swear deceitfully.
He will receive blessing from the
    Lord,
    and vindication from the God of
    his salvation.
Such is the generation of those who
    seek him,
    who seek the face of the God of
    Jacob.   24:1-6

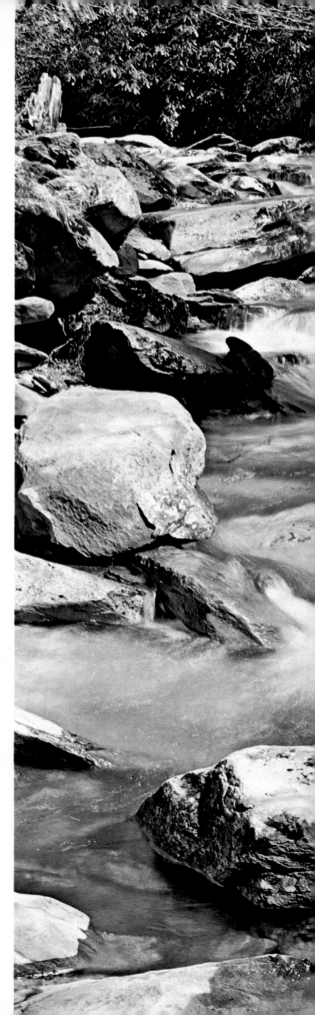

He divided the sea and let them
pass through it,
and made the waters stand like
a heap.
In the daytime he led them with a
cloud,
and all the night with a fiery
light.
He cleft rocks in the wilderness,
and gave them drink abundantly
as from the deep.
He made streams come out of the
rock,
and caused waters to flow down
like rivers.   78:13-16

Who turns the rock into a pool of
water,
the flint into a spring of water.   114:8

Thou visitest the earth and
waterest it,
thou greatly enrichest it;
the river of God is full of water;
thou providest their grain,
for so thou hast prepared it.
Thou waterest its furrows
abundantly,
settling its ridges,
softening it with showers,
and blessing its growth.   65:9,10

The pastures of the wilderness drip,
the hills gird themselves with joy,
the meadows clothe themselves
with flocks,

the valleys deck themselves with
grain,
they shout and sing together for
joy. 65:12,13

$$\mathbb{H}e \text{ gives snow like wool;}$$

He gives snow like wool;
  he scatters hoarfrost like ashes.
He casts forth his ice like morsels;
  who can stand before his cold?   147:16,17

29

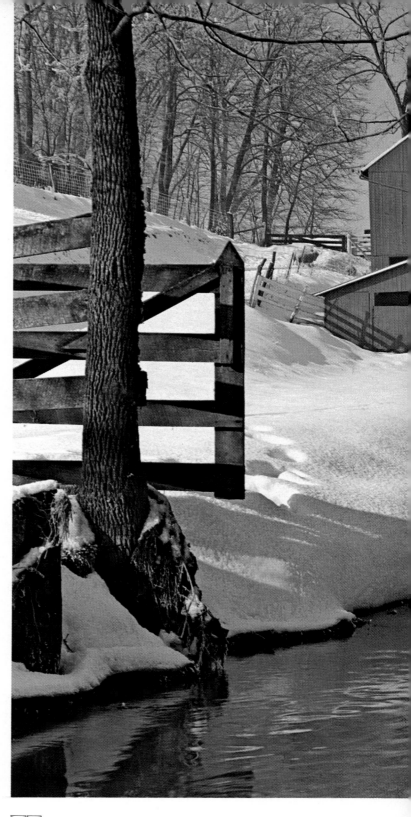

He sends forth his word, and melts
   them;
he makes his wind blow, and the
   waters flow.   147:18

BUT THE EARTH
HE HAS GIVEN
TO THE SONS OF MEN

Thou hast given him dominion over
 the works of thy hands;
  thou hast put all things under his
   feet,
all sheep and oxen,
 and also the beasts of the field   8:6,7

The birds of the air, and the fish of
 the sea,
whatever passes along the paths
 of the sea.   8:8

O Lord, our Lord,
how majestic is thy name in all
 the earth!   8:9

He covers the heavens with clouds,
  he prepares rain for the earth,
  he makes grass grow upon the
    hills.
He gives to the beasts their food,
  and to the young ravens which
    cry.   147:8,9

36

He makes peace in your borders;
he fills you with the finest of the
wheat.   147:14

They sow fields, and plant vineyards,
  and get a fruitful yield.
By his blessing they multiply
      greatly;
  and he does not let their cattle
      decrease.   107·37 38

The earth has yielded its increase;
  God, our God, has blessed us.
God has blessed us;
  let all the ends of the earth fear
      him!   67:6,7

The plowers plowed upon my back;
they made long their furrows. 129:3

I will sing to the Lord,
  because he has dealt bountifully
    with me. 13:6

May the Lord give you increase,
  you and your children!
May you be blessed by the Lord,
  who made heaven and earth!
The heavens are the Lord's
    heavens,
  but the earth he has given to the
    sons of men. 115:14-16

THE LORD
IS MY SHEPHERD

The Lord is my shepherd, I
shall not want;
he makes me lie down in green
pastures.   23:1,2

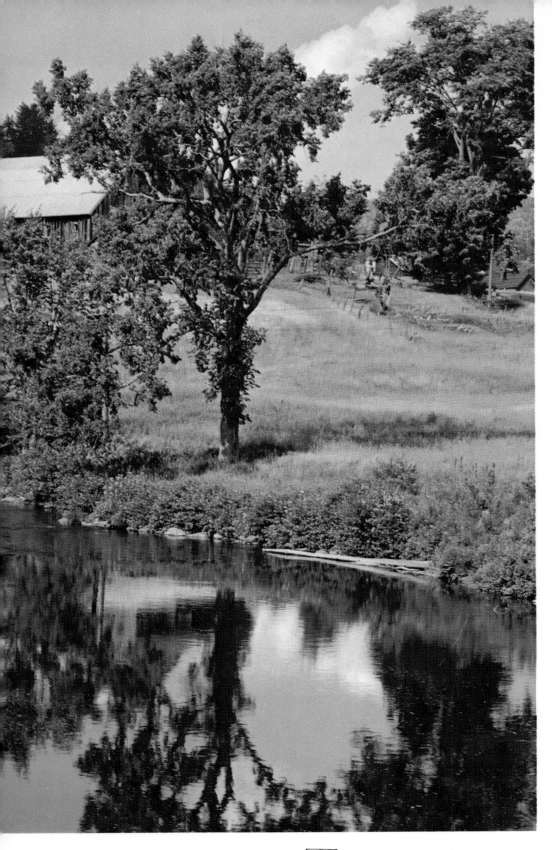

He leads me beside still waters   23:2

He restores my soul.
He leads me in paths of righteousness
for his name's sake.   23:3

Even though I walk through the
valley of the shadow
I fear no evil;
for thou art with me;
thy rod and thy staff,
they comfort me. 23:4

*Thou preparest a table before me
in the presence of my enemies;
thou anointest my head with oil,
my cup overflows.* 23:5

Surely goodness and mercy shall
follow me
all the days of my life;
and I shall dwell in the house of
the Lord
for ever.   23:6

GREAT IS HIS STEADFAST LOVE

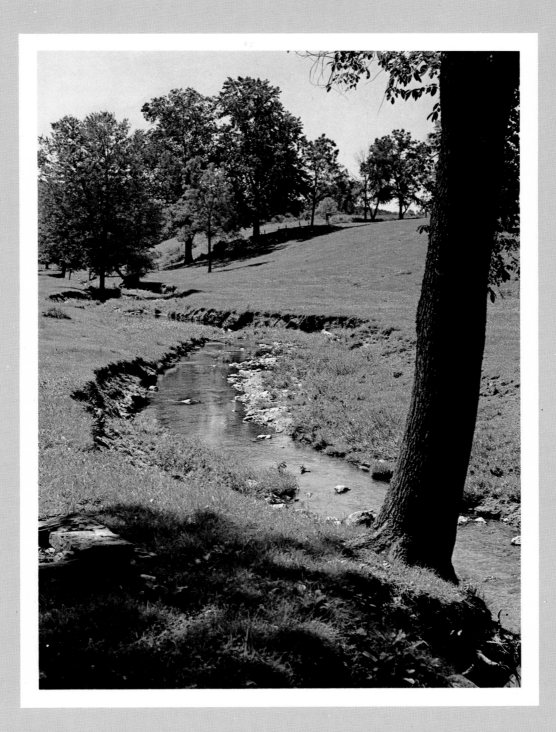

Blessed is the man
   who walks not in the counsel of
     the wicked,
nor stands in the way of sinners,
   nor sits in the seat of scoffers;
but his delight is in the law of the
     Lord,
   and on his law he meditates day
   and night.

He is like a tree
   planted by streams of water,
that yields its fruit in its season,
   and its leaf does not wither.
In all that he does, he prospers. *1:1-3*

As for man, his days are like grass;
   he flourishes like a flower of the
     field;
for the wind passes over it, and it
     is gone,
    and its place knows it no more.
But the steadfast love of the Lord
     is from everlasting to
     everlasting
    upon those who fear him,
    and his righteousness to
     children's children,
to those who keep his covenant
    and remember to do his
     commandments.   *103:15-18*

In thee, O Lord, do I seek
     refuge;
   let me never be put to shame;
   in thy righteousness deliver me!
Incline thy ear to me,
     rescue me speedily!
Be thou a rock of refuge for me,
     a strong fortress to save me!
Yea, thou art my rock and my
     fortress;
   for thy name's sake lead me and
     guide me   31:1-3

Thy steadfast love, O Lord,
   extends to the heavens,
  thy faithfulness to the clouds.
Thy righteousness is like the moun-
    tains of God,
  thy judgments are like the great
    deep;
man and beast thou savest,
    O Lord.   36:5,6

Know that the Lord is God!
It is he that made us, and we are
   his;
we are his people, and the sheep
   of his pasture.   *100:3*

Then we thy people, the flock of
   thy pasture,
will give thanks to thee for ever;
from generation to generation we
   will recount thy praise.   *79:13*

The Lord looks down from heaven,
   he sees all the sons of men;
from where he sits enthroned he
      looks forth
   on all the inhabitants of the
      earth,
he who fashions the hearts of them
     all,
   and observes all their deeds.   33:13-15

Behold, how good and
     pleasant it is
when brothers dwell in unity!   133:1

MANIFOLD
ARE
THY WORKS

Bless the Lord, O my soul!
  O Lord my God, thou art
    very great!

Thou art clothed with honor and
    majesty,
  who coverest thyself with light as
    with a garment,
who hast stretched out the heavens
    like a tent. . .

who makest the clouds thy chariot,
  who ridest on the wings of the
    wind,
who makest the winds thy
    messengers,
  fire and flame thy ministers.
Thou didst set the earth on its
    foundations,
  so that it should never be shaken. 104:1-5

The mountains rose, the valleys
    sank down
  to the place which thou didst
    appoint for them.
Thou didst set a bound which they
    should not pass,
  so that they might not again
    cover the earth.
Thou makest springs gush forth in
    the valleys. . .
they give drink to every beast of the
    field;
  the wild asses quench their thirst.
By them the birds of the air have
    their habitation;
  they sing among the branches. *104:8-12*

Thou dost cause the grass to grow
        for the cattle,
    and plants for man to cultivate,
that he may bring forth food from
        the earth. . .
The trees of the Lord are watered
        abundantly. . .
In them the birds build their nests;
    the stork has her home in the fir
        trees.
The high mountains are for the
        wild goats;
    the rocks are a refuge for the
        badgers.   104:14-18

Thou hast made the moon to mark
the seasons;
the sun knows its time for setting.
Thou makest darkness, and it is
night   104:19,20

When the sun rises. . .
Man goes forth to his work
and to his labor until the evening. 104:22,23

O Lord, how manifold are thy
   works! . . .
Yonder is the sea, great and wide,
   which teems with things
      innumerable,
   living things both small and
      great.   104:24,25

These all look to thee,
  to give them their food in due
    season.
When thou givest to them, they
    gather it up;
  when thou openest thy hand,
    they are filled with good
    things.
I will sing to the Lord as long as
    I live;
  I will sing praise to my God
    while I have being.
May my meditation be pleasing to
    him,
  for I rejoice in the Lord. . .
Bless the Lord, O my soul!
Praise the Lord!   104:27,28,33-35

I LIFT UP
MY EYES

Be still, and know that I am God.
I am exalted among the nations,
I am exalted in the earth!"
The Lord of hosts is with us;
the God of Jacob is our
refuge.   46:10,11

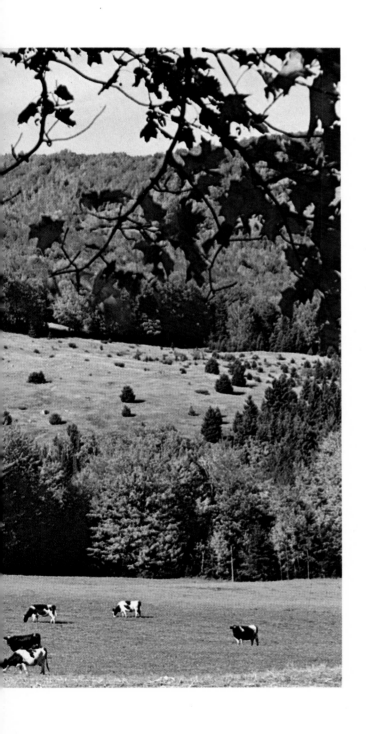

I *lift up my eyes to the hills.*
From whence does my help come?
My help comes from the Lord, who made heaven and earth. 121:1,2

Hear my cry, O God,
    listen to my prayer;
from the end of the earth I call to
    thee,
    when my heart is faint.
Lead thou me
    to the rock that is higher than I;
for thou art my refuge,
    a strong tower against the enemy.   61:1-3

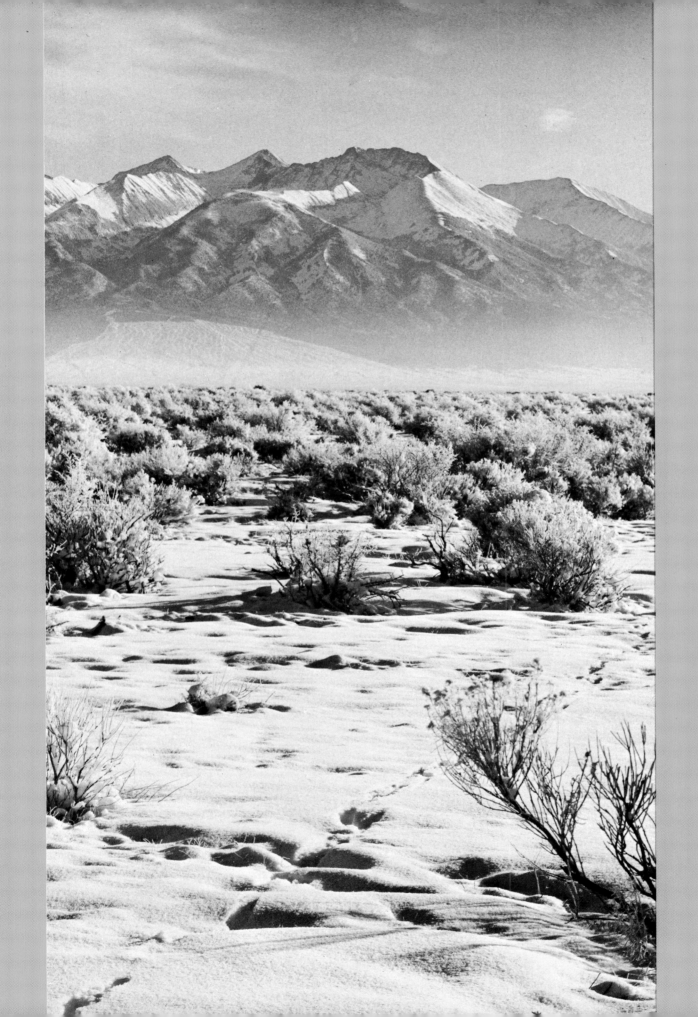

He made the storm be still,
and the waves of the sea were
hushed.
Then they were glad because they
had quiet,
and he brought them to their
desired haven.

Let them thank the Lord for his
steadfast love,
for his wonderful works to the
sons of men!
Let them extol him in the congre-
gation of the people,
and praise him in the assembly
of the elders.   107:29-32

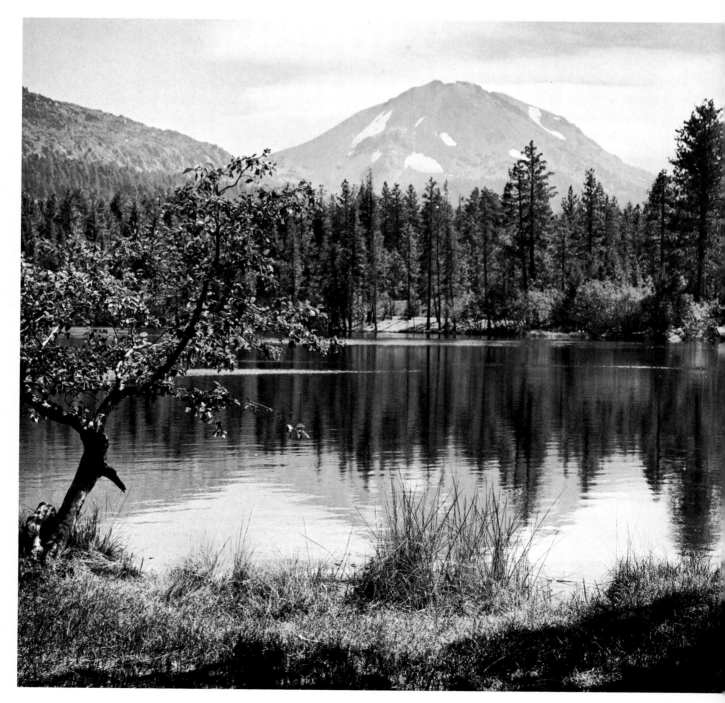

When peoples gather together,
and kingdoms, to worship the
Lord.   102:22

Let us go to his dwelling place;
let us worship at his footstool!"   132:7

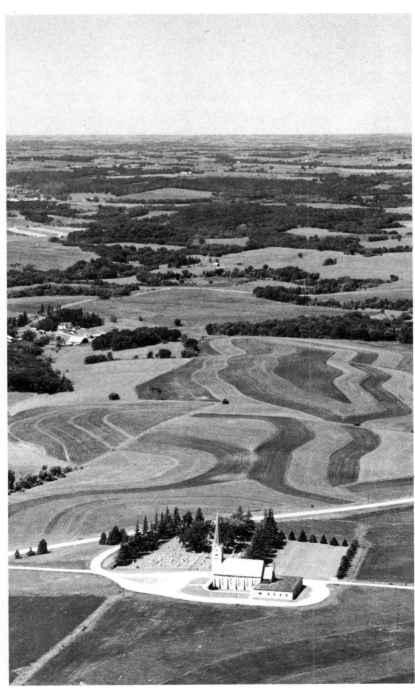

I was glad when they said
   to me,
"Let us go to the house of the
   Lord!"   122:1

But I through the abundance of thy
   steadfast love
will enter thy house,
I will worship toward thy holy
   temple   5:7

I will walk with integrity of heart
within my house;
I will not set before my eyes
anything that is base.   101:2,3

Let the words of my mouth and the
meditation of my heart
be acceptable in thy sight,
O Lord, my rock and my
redeemer.   19:14

PRAISE
THE LORD

Praise the Lord!
Praise, O servants
of the Lord,
praise the name
of the Lord!
Blessed be the name
of the Lord
from this time forth
and for evermore! 113,1-2

From the rising of the sun to its
   setting
  the name of the Lord is to be
    praised!
The Lord is high above all nations,
  and his glory above the heavens!   113:3-4